Bird
Watching

Colour
Library
Direct

CLD 21095
This edition published in 1998 for
Colour Library Direct
Godalming Business Centre
Woolsack Way
Godalming
Surrey GU7 1XW

ISBN: 1-85833-932-4

Printed in China

Produced by
Haldane Mason,
London

Acknowledgements
Art Director: Ron Samuels
Editor: Charles Dixon-Spain
Design: Zoë Mellors
Illustration: copyright Parragon except for those by Martin Woodcock, specifically, the *Red-legged Partridge*
(26, 59), the *Lapwing* (27, 59), the *Pied Flycatcher* (39, 60) and the *Cormorant* (50, 62) which are reproduced
courtesy of New Holland Publishing.

Picture acknowledgements: Bruce Coleman; 11 (Bob Glover), 13, 14 (George McCarthy),
24 (George McCarthy), 32 (Bob Glover), 42 (Dennis Green), 48 (Kim Taylor)

Contents

WHY BIRDWATCH?

Why do so many of us watch birds so enthusiastically? Perhaps the easiest answer, is that birds seem to be the commonest, most attractive and easiest observed wildlife around us, and simply add to the interest and pleasure of being alive. No matter where you are, at home, on a mountain-top, in mid-ocean or deep in a city, there are birds around, not simply to look at but to watch with interest. This interest may be in following their behaviour, or in seeing how their numbers change with the seasons, or in unravelling the challenges of a difficult identification problem. Birds can enliven the walk to school or to the station, and will add another dimension to a holiday at home or abroad. A detailed investigation of the birds around where you live can produce as many surprises and interesting discoveries as an overseas trip to a country with different scenery, vegetation and climate. No matter how keen and how skilful a birdwatcher you become, there will always be a pleasure in being among wild things, maybe as simple as observing a Robin hunting worms in the garden, Blue Tits squabbling over the best peanuts or Goldfinches extracting seeds from a prickly thistle.

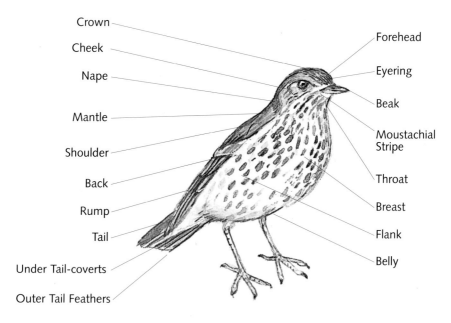

HOW TO USE THIS GUIDE

To help you find them more easily, the birds in this book are grouped into five habitat sections and within those sections into groups or families like the crows or the game birds. Because birds are so mobile, and will fly to find new food supplies, they can occur in more than one habitat, so we have used symbols alongside each bird's name to indicate where else you may find it. The symbols are:

town	farmland	woodland	heathland	freshwater

Each bird has its English name, and also its scientific name (see p15), a quick guide to its size and a more accurate length from beak to tail tip. Descriptions of its appearance, calls and song, where you can find it and how likely you are to see it (is it common or rare?) follow.

For each bird we have provided a distribution diagram, dividing Europe into four sections: northwest, southwest, southeast and northeast. These same distribution diagrams are just as useful if your birdwatching is restricted to Britain and Ireland. Depending on seasonal variation or absence there is a letter in each quarter showing the likelihood of seeing each bird.

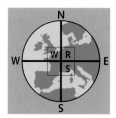

R	Resident
S	Summer Visitor
W	Winter Visitor
	Rarely Seen

If you are not sure which bird you have seen, and cannot readily identify it flicking through the book, refer to the quick-reference table at the end, which gives small pictures of all the birds you are likely to come across. And remember, part of the fun of birdwatching is that birds don't obey our rules: always keep your eyes and minds open . . .

THE LIVES OF BIRDS

Ask people what is special about being a bird, and most will answer 'they can fly'. Yes they can, and far better than any aeroplane we have designed, particularly when its comes to energy-efficiency and manoeuvrability. The shape of a bird's wings, and the way it flies, often provide the first clues to its identity. Other animals can fly (but not so well) including bats and millions upon millions of insects, so flight is not a unique bird feature. What is unique is a bird's covering of feathers. No other animal has them or anything like them.

Feathers are tough yet flexible, wind- and waterproof, and some (down feathers) are as good at keeping birds warm as a duvet is at keeping humans warm. The flight feathers in the wings are exceptionally strong, because they power the bird through the air. They can be colourful, so that a male can show off, or frighten away enemies, or perfectly camouflaged for concealment, like a female Mallard on her nest. Feathers grow from the bird's skin (like our hair) but wear out in time. Most birds, except the very largest, change their feathers once each year. This is called moult and takes place gradually (so that a bird is never completely naked and unable to fly!) over a couple of months, usually at the end of the summer.

A bird's year really begins in early spring. As the days get longer, males will begin to sing. This helps them attract a female as a mate, and also marks out the edges of the territory that the pair will need to raise their family. Territories can be less than three feet (one metre) across in colonial nesting birds like Rooks and are sometimes as large as 20 square miles (50 square kilometres) or more for a Raven on hill farmland.

Once the pair have established their relationship, nest building begins. Nest types vary and include simple saucer shapes scraped in the earth and lined with plant material, floating rafts of waterweed (the home of the Little Grebe) and finely woven nests containing over two thousand individual parts (like those made by the Chaffinch and the Long-tailed Tit).

Blue tit: feathered for all weather

And remember, birds make nests without the use of hands, which evolution formed into wings, and instead depend on beak and feet to make their ingenious homes.

In the nest the female lays her eggs, called a clutch. While some birds lay a single egg, a clutch usually numbers between four to six eggs, but as many as 15 are laid by ducks and tits. Some birds lay just one clutch each summer, others two, three or four. The nestlings that hatch after two to four weeks may leave the nest almost immediately, like ducklings, or stay, needing more time to develop feathers and strength. Some birds, like the Tawny Owl, look after and train their young to hunt over a period of three months after this.

Bird diets vary greatly. Some are vegetarian, others flesh-eating (carnivorous) or insectivorous, or a mixture depending on what is available. Carnivores have hooked beaks (owls and hawks), seed-eaters wedge-shaped beaks for crushing their food and insect-eaters finely pointed slender beaks to pick insects up effectively. Those with mixed diets, called omnivores, have beaks somewhere between.

We know that many birds are not with us all year round. The best example is the Swallow, arriving in spring, departing in autumn displaying what is one of birds' most amazing features, the ability to migrate. Many summer migrants like the Swallow feed on insects, and would not be able to survive our winter when no insects are about. Instead, they fly south to Africa in the autumn, where there are plenty of insects. We still do not know how they do this. Their journey is several thousand miles long, crosses the Sahara Desert, and yet is carried out with incredible navigational accuracy, despite many dangers along the way. In spring they return, usually to the same nesting place as the year before. All we can do is marvel at their skill.

Expert carpentry is not necessary to build a nestbox. Interior dimensions should be no less than 6 × 6 inches (15 × 15 cm), 8 inches (20 cm) deep with an entrance hole of 1 inch (3 cm) in diameter.

Bird tables are a great way of bringing birds into your garden, as well as helping them survive through periods of bad weather. Note the guard to stop cats and squirrels climbing up to attack the birds or steal the food.

ARRANGING THE BIRDS

Most birdwatchers find the number of birds illustrated in field guides bewildering. There are a lot, and many of them we may never see near home, but may find on holiday. To make things easier, we need to group types of bird together. In this book, we have taken five types of countryside – habitats – and grouped together the birds that you are most likely to see in them, which is a good way to do it for beginners.

Great Tit

House Sparrow

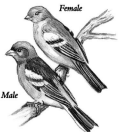

Female

Male

We can go further. Though birds seem to be very good at breaking the rules we try to apply, most families of birds tend to eat similar things – for example all pigeons and doves are vegetarian, all swallows and martins eat insects. Also, there are leg and beak adaptations to various ways of life – for example swimming birds like ducks or grebes have webbed feet or lobed toes, and birds of prey and owls have sharply hooked beaks to tear flesh into bite-sized chunks. Pointers like this all help you find your way around the world of birds.

WHAT IS A 'SPECIES'?

Chaffinches and Goldfinches are obviously related to each other – they have similar wedge-shaped beaks, similar feet and both eat seeds, but in the wild they never interbreed. We can recognize them from each other, and so can they. When it comes to the nesting season, a Chaffinch only recognizes the plumage colours of another Chaffinch, and the same is true for a Goldfinch. Also, habitat differences play their part in keeping the two separate: Chaffinches are woodland birds, Goldfinches like heath and scrub. When two types of birds like this, obviously related, never interbreed, we call each a species.

Goldfinch

Female

Male

Male and female Chaffinches (left) have different plumages, while male and female Goldfinches (above right) are very similar. Even the House Sparrow shows a marked differentiation between male and female plumages (above left).

8

NAMING THE BIRDS

When the earliest colonists went to America, they
saw a red-breasted thrush, and thinking of
home, called it 'robin'. It is much bigger and more

Grey Heron

Blackbird-like than the bird we call a Robin. To avoid this sort of
problem round the world, each bird is given two scientific names,
and the same ones are used everywhere in the world in books and
field guides – just as they are in this guide. You can get a clue to
relationships from these scientific names: for example, you would not
know that Blackbird, Mistle Thrush and Redwing were closely related
from their English names, but if you look, each is called *Turdus* as its first
scientific name, which means that each is a species in the genus *Turdus*.
The Mistle Thrush is called *Turdus viscivorus*. The second name is
its 'specific' name (like our Christian or given names), and often tells
you something about the bird. In the case of the Mistle Thrush, visci comes
from Viscum, the scientific name for mistletoe, whose berries Mistle Thrushes
love to eat, and vorus is Latin for 'eater'. So *Turdus viscivorus* = mistletoe-
eating thrush.

Related genera (the plural of genus) are grouped in families. World-wide out
of a grand total of about 8000 bird species, the
thrush family tops the list with a total of 1153.
Others in the 'top 15' include

Female

buntings (522 species), pigeons and doves (289),
hawks (217), woodpeckers (210), pheasants
(165) – surprisingly ahead of ducks (147).

Male

The Tufted Duck: one of the ducks that dive
expertly for their food.

9

THE GEAR

BINOCULARS

It is perfectly possible to see and enjoy birds without any special equipment, but a whole new world opens up to you once you have your first pair of binoculars, like those contained in this box set. Distant birds stop being little dots against the sky or water, and take on shapes and colours, while close-up views show that feathers have a real beauty of their own. Binoculars allow you to identify birds correctly, and give you a wonderful chance to spy on them going about their daily lives. However, never look directly at the sun using binoculars, because direct sunlight can hurt the eyes.

WHAT TO WEAR

Make sure always when you go birdwatching that your clothes are suitable for the weather (allowing for it to get worse!) and for the habitat you are visiting. Bare legs do not go well with gorse, nettles or brambles. As a general rule, it is better to pack a little too much clothing in a rucksack than risk getting cold and wet. In really hot weather, a hat of some sort is sensible. For cooler weather, a practical outfit would be jeans, a roll-neck sweater or fleece, and a weatherproof kagoul with a hood. A pair of lightweight waterproof overtrousers can be most useful in really wet weather. In midwinter a warmer, thicker waterproof is sensible, and don't forget gloves.

What you wear on your feet depends on how wet and cold it is. Trainers are often ideal, as in summer are basketball boots, which dry out much quicker if you get them wet. Really muddy winter walks are best tackled in wellingtons (remember thick warm socks), but overall, waterproof leather or fabric walking boots are the most comfortable and best for preventing sprained ankles. However, walking boots are expensive and need caring for properly.

WHERE AND WHEN

As the scenery and vegetation of our countryside varies from region to region with changing geology and climate, so too do the birds you can hope to see. Generally speaking, there are more species as you travel eastwards, fewer as you travel west towards Ireland. The number of different habitats in an area also plays a part. Far more birds will be present, for example, in a countryside of mixed farmland with hedges and woodland, than in large areas of open fields, or heathland, or even big woodlands. Just as there are specialist craftsmen and general workers among people, so there are specialist birds for almost every habitat, and 'general purpose' birds that can manage very well in a wide variety of surroundings.

Binoculars greatly increase the enjoyment of birdwatching. Here they are allowing one enthusiast watch rare birds of prey at Pointo de Sahun *in the Spanish Pyranees.*

FIELDCRAFT

Using binoculars is one way to bring birds closer to you, but another way of improving your birdwatching is to get nearer to them. If wild creatures are not made aware of your presence they will continue to behave naturally, and perhaps pass close by you. Fortunately, birds (unlike mammals) have no sense of smell – so we do not have to worry about the wind blowing our scent to them and frightening them. But all birds have keen eyesight, much better than ours. A hovering Kestrel can spot a beetle in the grass 120 feet (40 metres) below. Birds also have acute hearing: their lives and their ability to find food depend on these senses.

So what does the birdwatcher need to do? First, always move about quietly, do not give the birds advance warning of your arrival or they will move away. Practice the hunter's method of moving silently in woodland. Avoid crashing through the bushes, or snapping twigs and rotten branches underfoot. Pause frequently to listen: songs and calls will tell you what birds to expect to see. Few people realize how helpful a good knowledge of bird songs and calls can be. When you are in a wood one day, try counting separately the birds you see first and those you hear first. Birds have a whole series of calls, ranging from the contact 'here I am', that helps to keep a flock together, to a 'come-for-food' call. The alarm note is usually short and strident. Parent birds have special calls that they use to signal to their young, including a different, much softer, danger signal that means 'keep quiet and still, there is danger about'. The sooner you can identify the noises birds make, the better birdwatcher you will become, and the better sightings you will get.

Always walk slowly in good birdwatching country. Use the natural cover provided by banks, trees and bushes. Before you reach a gap, pause and listen for a few moments, and look around. Sometimes you should stand still for a while, and let the bird betray its presence by moving before you do. Do your best to avoid sudden movements – like whipping out a handkerchiek to blow your nose! Avoid wearing brightly-coloured clothing: most modern kagouls and anoraks are made in bright colours for safety reasons, so choose the least conspicuous dark blue or green, and try not to wear stiff materials that will crackle or scrape on twigs.

Always remember to put the birds' interests first. Do not crowd round a tired migrant, however 'tame' or however rare. If you find a fledgling out of the nest leave it where it is – it may look lost and pathetic, but there will be a parent nearby who can look after it much better than you can! Also, be careful not to disturb nesting birds. Lastly, remember other people may be birdwatching too. When you have finished looking, don't just stand up and walk away, scaring birds in all directions.

Hides provide excellent views of birds and protection from wind and rain. Nature reserves are a great place to get to know your birds – not only do the birds behave naturally, but you can refer to this guide book without the distractions of the elements.

TOWN

No other habitat has been as influenced by people as our villages, towns and cities. Though this may sound like bad news, many birds are able to live contentedly right among us. Gardeners have brought plants from all over the world to make their gardens more beautiful – these have berries or seeds (often bigger than the wild ones) and our insects are quite at home on them – so there is plenty of food. Many species of birds have adapted well to this habitat, braving dangers like our cats and cars. Even big cities are not the barren concrete canyons without birdlife: city parks with their lakes, churchyards and playing fields, all encourage birds.

For the birdwatcher, our houses are ready-made hides, the birds are tamer, and we can tempt them even closer with nestboxes and bird baths in summer, and with bird feeders in winter, letting us share their daily lives.

HERRING GULL *Larus argentatus*
Large: 55 cm

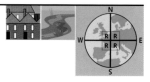

Typical gull: adults have white head and body, pale silver-grey back. In flight shows black wingtips with white markings. Beak yellow with red spot near tip. Legs and webbed feet distinctively pink. Immatures are mottled white and brown above, paler below, becoming white after 3 years.
Call: mewing cries like a cat; harsh 'kyow' calls accelerating into a noisy laugh.

Where? Can be seen almost anywhere at any time of year. Often feeds on rubbish tips, rests on reservoirs or fields. Common.

LESSER BLACK-BACKED GULL *Larus fuscus*
Large: 53 cm

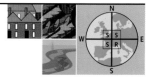

Typical gull: adults have white head and body, slate-grey back. In flight shows black wingtips with small white marks. Beak yellow with red spot at tip. Legs and webbed feet yellow. Immatures are mottled white and brown above, paler below, not greatly different from young Herring Gulls. Adult plumage comes gradually over 3 years.
Call: mewing cries and laughing 'kyow' calls like Herring Gull.

Where? Mostly a summer visitor, but increasingly common in winter. Visits rubbish tips, reservoirs, playing fields; more often seen on farmland than Herring Gull, especially spring and autumn. Fairly common.

GREAT BLACK-BACKED GULL *Larus marinus*
Large: 68 cm

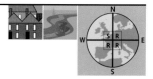

Typical gull, obviously larger than Herring Gull. Adults have white head and body, jet black back. In flight, wings show white trailing edge and white spots at tips. Beak large and strong, yellow with red spot near tip. Legs and webbed feet distinctively pink. Immatures mottled brown and white, take 4 years to reach adult plumage.

Call: usually silent, occasional deep gruff 'kow-kow-kow'.
Where? A real sea gull, but visits rubbish tips all year round, resting on reservoirs and town playing fields. Scarcer than other gulls.

BLACK-HEADED GULL *Larus ridibundus*
Medium: 35 cm

Typical gull, obviously smaller than Herring Gull. Adults in summer have white body, dark brown head and pale grey back. Beak, legs and dark red webbed feet. In flight wings show characteristic white leading edge and black-tipped white wingtips. Adults in winter have white heads with a sooty smudge behind the eye. Immatures show a brown stripe on the wing and have a black-tipped white tail.

Call: very noisy; cackling and laughing 'yelps'.
Where? Almost anywhere right through the year. Feed on rubbish tips, often seen in town parks and on playing fields, and on farmland, particularly newly ploughed. Common.

WOODPIGEON *Columba palumbus*
Medium: 39 cm

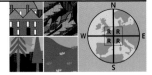

Largest pigeon with characteristic large body and small head and neck. Grey body, grey-brown back and wings, often looks pinkish on breast. Adults have striking white and metallic green patches on sides of neck, absent in immatures. Beak red with yellow tip, legs dark pink. Flight often clumsy and noisy on rounded wings, showing diagnostic white crescent-shaped bar.

Call: monotonous and penetrating 'coo-coo, coo-coo' with emphasis on second syllable.
Where? Almost anywhere right through the year. Often becomes very tame in town parks. Common.

COLLARED DOVE *Streptopelia decaocto*
Medium: 28 cm

Smaller and slimmer than Woodpigeon; sandy buff above, paler and pinker on underparts. White-edged black collar round back of neck, absent in immatures. In flight shows grey wings with brown flight feathers, and brown tail with broad white tip on underside. Black beak, red legs.
Call: rasping sigh on landing; monotonous 'coo-coo-coo' song.

Where? Almost any town or village year-round, also farms with cereal crops or chickens. Only arrived in Britain for the first time in 1955, but has spread like wildfire to be common everywhere.

SWIFT *Apus apus*
Small: 18 cm

Almost always seen in flight. Sooty black all over apart from slightly paler throat. Torpedo-shaped body, distinctive long, slim curved wings and flickering flight. Tail short, notched. Legs and beak tiny, eyes large. Often in groups swooping between buildings. Eats, sleeps and drinks on the wing, landing only to enter nest holes under roof.

Call: shrill screaming.
Where? Summer visitor to many towns and cities. Often travels to feed over lakes and reservoirs, particularly in wet weather. Often common.

SWALLOW *Hirundo rustica*
Small: 20 cm

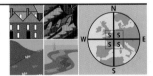

Familiar summer visitor. Glossy blue-black above, with chestnut face and blackish throat. Underparts whitish. Distinctive long curved wings, and deeply forked tail. Slim tail streamers (outermost tail feathers) longer in male than female – both longer than in immatures. Tail feathers show white spots when banking and turning. Often seen in flight, also perches on overhead wires.

Call: 'chirrup' in alarm; extended twittering song.
Where? Widespread almost everywhere except in town centres, often common.

HOUSE MARTIN *Delichon urbica*
Tiny: 12 cm

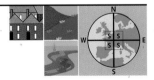

Familiar summer visitor, building distinctive cup-shaped nests of mud pellets under the eaves of buildings. Dumpy and short-winged compared with Swallow, glossy blue-black above with black wings, brilliant white below. Short blackish tail with shallow notch, separated from back by white rump patch. Beak black, legs and feet tiny, covered in white feathers. Collects mud pellets from edges of puddles. Often in groups.
Call: sharp 'chip' of alarm; chattering unmusical song.
Where? Many (but not all) towns and villages will have House Martin colonies. Fairly common.

PIED WAGTAIL *Motacilla alba*
Small: 18 cm

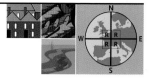

Typical wagtail, with small plump body, long slender legs and long tail which never stops wagging up and down. Male in summer black above, white below, but with white face markings and a large black bib. Wings black with bold white markings, black tail with white edges. Winter male, female and immature duller and greyer. Flight swooping and fluttery. Runs fast chasing insect food.

Call: twittering featureless song, but very distinctive and regularly used sharp 'chis-ick' call.
Where? Year-round resident in town parks, especially close to ponds or lakes; playing fields, close to freshwater and on farmland anywhere. Fairly common.

WREN *Troglodytes troglodytes*
Tiny: 10 cm

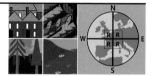

Almost spherical with a distinctive vertically-cocked tail. Rich chestnut-brown with darker barring, paler below than above. Slim curved and pointed beak, relatively strong brown legs, scuffles about on the ground under cover for long periods. Flights usually short and low, whirring along on short rounded wings.

Call: sings frequently, astonishingly loud musical song; scolding alarm 'churr'.
Where? Fairly common year-round in parks and gardens with plenty of undergrowth or low plants, in woodland and on farmland.

DUNNOCK *Prunella modularis*
Small: 15 cm

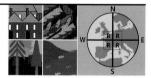

Looks dull and drab, but close-to beautifully patterned. Mottled browns and blacks above, with dark grey head and breast, paler grey-buff on belly. Short thin beak. Spends much time on the ground, usually close to undergrowth. Hops, always flicking wings and tail.
Call: loud and distinctive 'tseek' call, often from several birds at the end of the day. Brief but melodious song.
Where? Fairly common year-round in parks and gardens with plenty of undergrowth and low plants, in woodland and in farmland hedges and copses.

ROBIN *Erithacus rubecula*
Tiny: 13 cm

Familiar 'redbreast' of Christmas cards. Plump and perky, with long slender legs, short slim pointed beak. Adult sandy-buff above, with distinctive red face, throat and breast, surrounded by grey margin. Belly whitish. Immatures have characteristic shape, brown with bold buff spots. Often becomes tame.
Call: sharp 'tick' of alarm; musical high-pitched song throughout the

summer and on warm autumn and winter days.
Where? Common year-round in parks and gardens with plenty of undergrowth or low plants, in woodland and on farmland.

BLACKBIRD *Turdus merula*
Small: 25 cm

Large long-tailed thrush, familiar everywhere. Male glossy jet black all over, with striking, fairly strong orange beak and yellow eye-ring. Females are brown, paler and faintly streaked below, with a dark-bordered whitish throat. Immatures are dark reddish brown, dark-spotted on the underparts, buff on the back. Often tame.
Call: strident and distinctive 'chink' call; beautiful melodious

song, often given from a song-perch with a wide view.
Where? Common year-round in parks and gardens everywhere, and in woodland and on farmland.

SONG THRUSH *Turdus philomelos*
Small: 22 cm

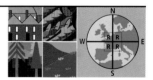

Familiar; shorter-tailed, smaller and more upright than Blackbird. Male and female similar, olive-brown above, whitish below with characteristic dark brown spots. Shows pale chestnut underwing in flight, reddish in Redwing. Immature similar, but with pale flecks on brown back. Often tame.
Call: 'tseep' call frequently given; song of characteristically simple

fluting notes, each repeated two to four times.
Where? Common year-round in parks and gardens everywhere, though usually less numerous than Blackbird. Also in woodland and on farmland.

MISTLE THRUSH *Turdus viscivorus*
Medium: 27 cm

Largest and palest of the thrushes. Upperparts pale grey-brown, underparts whitish with lots of large blackish spots. Immature even paler and greyer, with scaly markings on back. Flight distinctively swooping, with bursts of wingbeats followed by pause, showing characteristic white underwing and whitish sides to long grey-brown tail.
Call: rattling 'rrrrrr . . .' of alarm; slow, simple but melodic song, often produced early in the New Year on warmer days.
Where? Likes the open spaces of town parks and playing fields and larger gardens, also woods and farmland. Widespread, often in ones and twos, never as numerous as other thrushes.

BLUE TIT *Parus caeruleus*
Tiny: 12 cm

Familiar and tame garden and woodland bird. Greenish back with bright blue wings and tail. Crown blue, face white with black line through eye and black bib. Underparts yellow. Males brighter coloured than females. Immatures are yellower and duller overall. Acrobatic feeder on twigs, bird feeders.
Call: 'tsee-tsee-tsee-tsit'; the song itself is a fast trill following the opening 'tsee' notes.
Where? Likes town parks and gardens of any size, but can be seen almost anywhere, almost anytime, but rarely high in mountains or on exposed coasts. Often in flocks in winter. Common.

GREAT TIT *Parus major*
Small: 15 cm

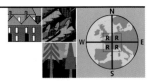

Largest European tit, with short stout beak, often feeds on the ground. Boldly patterned with green back, blue-grey wings, white-edged black tail and yellow underparts. Males have a bold black stripe down the centre of breast and belly, much less distinct in females. Characteristic black head with white cheek patches and a small white patch on the nape. Immatures duller and yellower.
Call: very varied, often 'tea-cher' or 'chink'. Song equally varied, loud, often based on 'tea-cher' notes.
Where? Year-round resident, in town, woods or on farmland. Regular at bird tables. Common, but not as numerous as Blue Tit.

STARLING *Sturnus vulgaris*
Small: 22 cm

Familiar noisy and aggressive year-round resident in parks and gardens. Blackish plumage glistens with green and purple sheens in summer, usually duller and buff-speckled in winter. Male has bristly throat feathers when singing. Short-tailed, with distinctive triangular wings in flight. Immature uniformly dull brown. Often in flocks, sometimes huge ones in winter.
Call: expert mimic of other birds, telephones etc. Harsh shrieking

call, song varied, partly musical, partly jangling.
Where? Likes town parks, playing fields and gardens of any size, but can be seen almost anywhere, at almost anytime of year. A regular bird-table visitor during the winter months. Common.

MAGPIE *Pica pica*
Medium: 45 cm

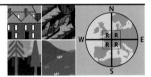

Unmistakable and familiar member of the crow family, with plump black and white body and long tapered black tail glistening green and purple in the sun (the tail makes up half its length). Short, rounded wings and long tail give distinctive fluttering, swooping fight. Builds characteristic large spherical twiggy nest high in a tree.

Call: harsh chattering cries; quiet musical song rarely heard.
Where? Only recently common in town parks and gardens, otherwise a farmland and woodland bird. Year-round resident, fairly common.

JACKDAW *Corvus monedula*
Medium: 33 cm

Smallest of the crow family, jaunty, sooty black all over apart from a grey face and nape and distinctive white eyes. Short wedge-shaped black beak, walks with rather long strides for its size. Often in flocks, often nests in holes in buildings.
Call: vocal, especially in flocks, sharp 'jack' calls.

Where? Year-round resident in towns and on farmland and elsewhere. Often quite common.

HOUSE SPARROW *Passer domesticus*
Small: 15 cm

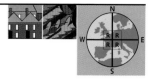

Familiar in cities, towns and villages and around even isolated buildings lived in by people. Male has characteristic brown-edged grey crown and black bib; streaked brown back and pale grey cheeks and underparts. Females and immatures are mottled buffs and browns above, paler below. Beak wedge-shaped. Often in flocks.
Call: noisy, continuous well-known 'chirrup' calls; song a series of unmusical 'chirrups' and 'squawks'.
Where? Year-round almost everywhere there are people, but favours towns, villages and farmyards. Common.

CHAFFINCH *Fringilla coelebs*
Small: 15 cm

Familiar finch with striking double white wingbars visible when perched and in flight. Male has brown back, grey head with black forehead, pink underparts, all duller in winter than summer. Wings black with white bars, tail black with white edges. Female and immature brown above, paler below, with the same distinctive wing and tail pattern. Often in flocks in winter.

Call: 'pink' call; song a descending cascade of musical notes with a final flourish.
Where? Widespread and common year-round. Enjoys town gardens, but just as at home in woodland and on farmland.

GREENFINCH *Carduelis chloris*
Small: 15 cm

Robust olive-green finch with large pinkish wedge-shaped beak. Males have grey heads, yellow underparts and shoulders, and bright yellow patches on each side of the base of the tail. Female and immature are duller.
Call: drawling 'dwee-eee' call; purring song produced while circling overhead with slow-motion wingbeats.

Where? Town parks and gardens year-round, will visit even the smallest garden with a peanut holder in winter. Also woodland and farmland, often in flocks in winter. Generally common.

SISKIN *Carduelis spinus*
Tiny: 12 cm

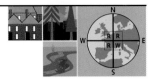

Like a small, slim and dark Greenfinch. Male green above with heavy black streaks, with yellow underparts and small black bib. Female and immature browner and duller. All show deeply forked tail (especially in flight), double yellow wingbars and yellow patches at the base of the tail. Small stubby beak. Sometimes in flocks.
Call: high-pitched 'twee-ooo' in flight; drawn-out jangling song.

Where? Visit graden peanut holders in winter, also waterside alder trees. Nests in conifer plantations. Not common, so a good spot.

GOLDFINCH *Carduelis carduelis*
Tiny: 13 cm

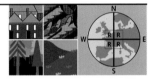

Unmistakable multicoloured finch with relatively long white wedge-shaped beak. Brown back, white-spotted black tail, white rump patch and underparts, black head with white cheeks and diagnostic red face (absent in immatures). In flight shows broad gold wingbars. Often in flocks.
Call: high-pitched 'dee-dee-litt' call; warbling jangling song.

Where? Year-round visitor to suburban and village gardens, less usual in town centres, also heath and farmland. Loves any open space especially with thistles. Generally pretty common.

NUTHATCH *Sitta europea*
Small: 15 cm

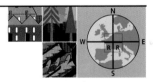

Like a mini-woodpecker, but short-tailed and climbs head-down as well as head-up. Grey above, pale chestnut below, redder on flanks in male. Relatively long dagger-like beak; black line through eye, white cheeks. Often solitary or in pairs.
Call: ringing 'chewit' call; loud 'too-wee, too-wee' song.

Where? Year-round resident in deciduous woodland and parks with tall trees. Visits garden bird tables in winter. Not found everywhere, but not uncommon in some areas. Always worth finding.

FARMLAND

As the number of people in Europe has increased, so has the need for farmland to grow the food they need. The first farm fields were just clearings in the huge forests of long ago, but until quite recently, wood was needed for building and for fires to keep houses warm, so patches of woodland, copses and spinneys were left and are still dotted around our farmland. The farmers needed boundaries to their fields, often to stop their sheep and cows from straying, so they made thick hedges.

Hedges work like the pipes from a reservoir, except that they spread birds from woods (and other animals and plants), not water, around the countryside. Many woodland birds are just as happy on farmland, which makes it great for birdwatching. Only when woods are chopped down and hedges torn out to make bigger fields do the birds, and birdwatchers, suffer.

PINK-FOOTED GOOSE *Anser brachyryhnchus*
Large: 65 cm

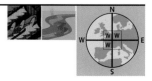

Small, neat, dark-bodied 'grey goose'. Body brown, paler on breast and white undertail. Neck very dark, head and beak small. Beak dark with pink markings, legs pink. In flight shows characteristic grey on wings. Usually in flocks.
Call: always noisy; distinctive high-pitched 'wink' calls.

Where? Winter visitor to farmland and also marshes, sometimes roosting overnight on nearby lakes. Often returns to same areas winter after winter, can be quite common.

WHITE-FRONTED GOOSE *Anser albifrons*
Large: 70 cm

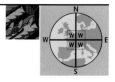

Commonest really wild goose in the south. Brown, white under tail. Adults have black bars on breast and conspicuous white faces absent in immatures. Legs orange. Beak orange in northern birds (from Greenland), pink in those further south (from Russia). Normally in flocks.
Call: noisy, distinctive and continuous puppy-like yelping.

Where? Winter visitor to farmland and also marshes, usually near the coast, but not always. Often returns to same areas year after year; can be quite common.

GREYLAG GOOSE *Anser anser*
Large: 80 cm

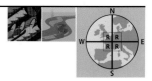

Largest 'grey goose' and ancestor of farmyard geese. Paler grey-brown than other grey geese and more heavily built. Pale pink feet conspicuous. Western birds have orange beaks, eastern ones pink. In flight looks heavy, shows pale blue-grey forewings. Often in flocks.
Call: noisy cackling just like farmyard geese.

Where? Genuinely wild birds winter on farmland and nearby moors and marshes. Some breed by Scottish lochs. In many areas resident populations descended from released captive stock are on the increase, usually close to water.

KESTREL *Falco tinnunculus*
Medium: 35 cm

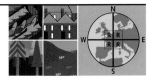

Has a falcon's long slender wings and tail, but also the distinctive habit of hovering, looking for prey below. Male has chestnut back and grey tail with black bar near tip, female and immature brown above, mottled black, buff below with black streaks. Usually solitary. **Call:** 'kee-kee-kee' and 'kree-ee-ee' calls in breeding season, silent at other times.

Where? Year-round farmland resident, often seen close to roads. Has also adapted well to living in towns. Common but not numerous.

RED-LEGGED PARTRIDGE *Alectoris rufa*
Medium: 35 cm

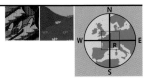

Plump, small-headed game bird with whirring flight low over the ground, but more often runs quietly away. Brown above, grey below with bold black, white and chestnut bars on flanks. White stripe over eye; black-edged white throat and bib of black speckles. Short strong beak and strong red legs. In pairs, occasionally small groups (coveys).

Call: often heard before seen – distinctive 'chuck, chuck-arr'. **Where?** Year-round on open farmland, also heathland. Widespread and fairly common.

GREY PARTRIDGE *Perdix perdix*
Medium: 30 cm

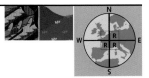

Plump, small-headed and upright game bird. Looks drab at a distance, beautifully marked close-to. Mottled and streaked grey-brown above, with chestnut face. Chestnut bars on side and black inverted 'U' on belly, less obvious in female. Flies low and fast on downturned rounded wings. Jumps into flight if disturbed but usually runs. In pairs or groups (coveys).

Call: easily separated from Red-legged by 'cheer-ick' calls. **Where?** Year-round farmland resident, also heathland. Widespread but irregular, numbers falling, often quite scarce.

QUAIL *Coturnix coturnix*
Small: 18 cm

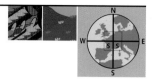

Dumpy, smallest game bird. Secretive, more often heard than seen. Brown above with black bars and white streaks, buff below. Male has striking black and white head pattern, obscure in female and immature. Usually solitary. **Call:** good ventriloquist, difficult to locate calls. Distinctive 'quit, quit-quit' or 'pit, pit-it' calls.

Where? Summer visitor to open farmland fields, usually grass or cereals. Numbers vary from year to year, scarce to rare. A good find.

PHEASANT *Phasianus colchicus*
Large: male 90 cm
female 60 cm

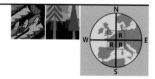

Male unmistakable: colourful, long-tailed game bird. Bronze body with black marks, blackish belly. Green head (often with white collar), fleshy red face patches, white beak. Female and immature well camouflaged in buff and brown. All have long tails which usually measure half their total size. Flies on whirring downcurved wings. Often in flocks, but often also raised for shooting.

Call: distinctive wing-claps follow male's ringing 'cork-cork' call. **Where?** Year-round resident in farmland and nearby woodland and scrub. Reasonably common.

LAPWING *Vanellus vanellus*
Medium: 30 cm

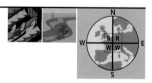

Member of the wader or shore bird family that has adapted to life on farmland. Upperparts blackish with a green sheen, underparts white with a black breast band and pale chestnut undertail. Black and white head with long slim upturned crest. Short black beak. Round-winged and very floppy in flight, flickering black and white. Often in flocks.

Call: distinctive 'pee-wit'. **Where?** Widespread on farmland, particularly grass or ploughed fields, year-round in the north, mostly in winter in the south. Fairly common.

COMMON GULL *Larus canus*
Medium: 40 cm

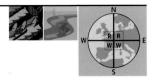

Typical gull, adult with white head and body, silver-grey back. In flight shows black wingtips with white spots. Beak and legs yellowish green. Immature pale brown above, whitish below, dark-streaked head. Often seen in flocks, and especially, following a ploughing tractor.
Call: 'kee-ow' and whining 'klee-oo'.

Where? Open farmland, particularly grassy fields. Breeds on farmland, nearby heaths and lakesides in the north, visits southern farms in spring and autumn on migration. Not uncommon.

BARN OWL *Tyto alba*
Medium: 35 cm

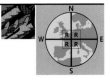

Ghostly white owl, sadly less common than it used to be. Upright stance, long-legged and knock-kneed, shows heart-shaped white face disc and large dark eyes. Underparts white, back sandy brown with fine markings. Long-winged in flight. Hunts at night, sometimes in daylight in winter. Usually solitary.

Call: frightening scream; snores at nest or when roosting.
Where? Widespread farmland bird year-round, but generally scarce. A wonderful sight.

LITTLE OWL *Athene noctua*
Small: 23 cm

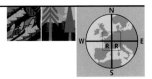

Smallest owl, upright and square headed. More often seen in daylight than other owls, will glare at you with yellow eyes and bob up and down on its perch. Brown above with large white spots, white below with bold dark streaks. Swooping flight on rounded wings. Usually solitary.

Call: various puppy-like yelps; far-carrying 'poo-oop'.
Where? Year-round farmland resident, also woodland. Numbers vary, not uncommon in places.

SKYLARK *Alauda arvensis*
Small: 18 cm

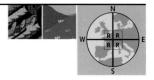

Well camouflaged on the ground, but easy to spot hovering and singing without a pause high over the fields. Brown above with paler and darker blotches, grey-buff underparts with brown streaks on breast. Greyish stripe over eye, short crest raised when excited. Shows dark tail with white outer feathers in flight. Usually solitary in summer, flocks in winter.

Call: rich 'chirrup' in flight. Continuous varied song in hovering flight, often imitates other birds.

Where? Year-round resident on farmland, also heath, favours wide-open fields of grass or cereals.

FIELDFARE *Turdus pilaris*
Small: 25 cm

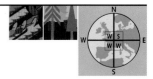

Large, long-tailed handsome thrush. Grey head, distinctive reddish-brown back, grey rump and black tail conspicuous in flight. Underparts buff, heavily dark speckled. Hesitant flight, several wingbeats followed by a swooping glide. Usually in flocks.
Call: very distinctive series of laughing or chuckling 'chack' calls; scratchy warbling song rarely heard.

Where? Open fields on farmland everywhere, sometimes through the winter or only during autumn and spring on migration. Quite common. Nests in the north.

REDWING *Turdus iliacus*
Small: 20 cm

Small thrush, Song Thrush-sized, but darker brown above, with red on flanks, showing as red underwings in flight. Distinctive white eyestripes and moustachial streaks, dark cheeks. Underparts whitish with dense dark streaking. Usually in flocks.
Call: thin 'see-eep' in flight, higher pitched and longer than Song Thrush. Slow simple flute-like song.

Where? Open fields and farmland everywhere, also woodland. Quite common in winter, but sometimes only on migration, autumn and spring. Nests in the north.

RAVEN *Corvus corax*
Large: 64 cm

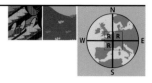

Largest of the crow family. All-black, with distinctively massive beak and long diamond-shaped tail. At close range large head and bristling throat feathers can be seen. Loves aerobatics, tumbling about in mid-air, swooping and diving. Solitary or in small groups. **Call:** gruff 'croaks', particularly deep 'gronk'.

Where? Farmland, particularly in the hills, near the moor and heathland or near the coast, often where there are sheep. Year-round resident, regular but not common: a good spot.

ROOK *Corvus frugilegus*
Medium: 45 cm

Glossy black crow with whitish dagger-shaped beak and fleshy face patches, absent in immatures. Strides around on grass showing 'baggy trouser' legs. Loves aerobatics on rounded wings, shows rounded tail. Almost always in flocks.
Call: noisy, 'carr' calls higher-pitched than Carrion/Hooded Crow.

Where? Widespread year-round on farmland, favours ploughed or grassy fields. Nests in noisy colonies in tall trees. Common.

CARRION/HOODED CROW *Corvus corone*
Medium: 45 cm

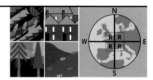

Two versions of the same bird: the all-black Carrion Crow lives in the south, the grey and black Hooded further north and west. Walks sedately, showing slim leg feathering (*see* Rook); tail square-ended in flight. Powerful black beak. Often solitary or in twos, only sometimes in flocks.
Call: deep 'caw' (deeper and harsher than Rook).

Where? Year-round on farmland everywhere. The Carrion Crow has also adapted well to town life. Fairly common.

BRAMBLING *Fringilla montifringilla*
Small: 15 cm

Male at end of winter unmistakable with orange breast, belly and shoulders, contrasting black head and wings. White rump patch. Earlier, male is duller in browns and orange, as are females and immatures. All show the white rump in flight. Often in flocks.
Call: distinctive 'tchway'.

Where? Farmland in winter, particularly stubble fields. Also loves feeding under beech trees. Numbers vary greatly year to year, widespread but only occasionally common.

BULLFINCH *Pyrrhula pyrrhula*
Small: 15 cm

Male distinctive, with reddish pink underparts, black cap, grey back and purplish black wings and tail. Female brownish buff with black cap, immature similar but lacks cap. All show distinctive white rump patch in flight. Shy and unobtrusive. Usually in ones or twos.
Call: soft but far-carrying 'pee-oo' whistle. Quiet creaking warbling song rarely heard.

Where? Widespread year-round on farmland, in orchards and in woodland, but not very common and good to see.

CORN BUNTING *Milaria calandra*
Small: 18 cm

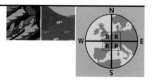

Perhaps the least musical and least attractively plumaged bird in Europe. Relatively large and plump, brown, slightly paler above than below, with darker spots and streaks. Wedge-shaped beak. In flight tail does not have the white sides usual in buntings. Solitary or in small groups.
Call: 'tsip' or 'tsip-ipp' in flight; distinctive metallic jangling song,

often referred to as 'like shaking nails in a tin can', usually given from a conspicuous perch.
Where? Widespread but erratic year-round resident on open farmland, also heathland. Not uncommon in some areas.

WOODLAND

Woodland, or more correctly forest, would have covered almost all of our landscape about 2000 years ago. Much has changed as towns and farmland have spread, and few real large forests remain in Europe. However, many woodland birds actually prefer the edges and clearings in our woods, so overall our losses have not been too great.

Even today, large woodlands and particularly dense plantations of conifers have fewer birds and can be rather dull for birdwatching. In woodland, birdwatching is difficult: nowhere else is moving quietly and slowly more important, nor getting to know bird songs and calls so that you can hear what is coming before it hears you.

Our woods provide plenty of plant and animal food for birds, an abundance of nest sites in summer, and shelter from snow and cold winds, especially over a long winter night.

STOCK DOVE *Columba oenas*
Medium: 33 cm

Typical dove with small head and bulky body, closely resembles typical town or racing pigeon. Grey overall, with pinkish flush on breast and metallic green neck patches. Black spots on closed grey-brown wings. Distinctively compact and fast in flight, showing black-edged grey triangular wings. Legs pink, beak pink with yellow tip. Immature duller, lacks neck spots. Sometimes in flocks.

Call: booming 'coo-oooh'.
Where? Year-round resident in woods and farmland nearby, nests in holes in trees. Fairly common.

TURTLE DOVE *Streptopelia turtur*
Medium: 28 cm

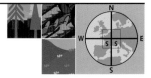

Smallest and smartest of the pigeons/doves. Blackish back feathers broadly edged gold: looks bronze above. Underparts pinkish buff, white on belly. Distinctive black and white check collar band on adults only. In flight shows blackish tail with narrow white edges (*see* Collared Dove). Rarely flocks.
Call: characteristic continuous 'prrrrr. . . .'

Where? Summer visitor to woodland and nearby farmland, often seen picking up grit from roads. Not very common.

TAWNY OWL *Strix aluco*
Medium: 38 cm

Familiar round-headed 'brown owl', nocturnal and heard more often than seen. Brown or chestnut above, finely streaked and blotched in black and buff. Underparts buff with black streaks. Face with two black-edged discs round dark eyes, two white 'eyebrows' stretching up onto crown. Usually solitary.

Call: 'too-whit-too-whoo', 'hoo-hoo-hooooo' or 'koo-wit'.
Where? Year-round woodland resident, less usual in conifers than deciduous woodland, also parks, even in city centres, and farmland. Widespread but not numerous.

LONG-EARED OWL *Asio otus*
Medium: 35 cm

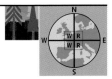

Secretive and well camouflaged. Brown above marked with black, buff and white, ginger below with black streaks. Buff discs round fiery golden eyes, two long tufts of feathers (the 'ears', but nothing to do with hearing) on forehead. Nocturnal and usually solitary. **Call:** usually the best way of finding them in the breeding season: a series of low 'poops', occasional 'kee-ee'.

Where? Year-round in some areas, winter visitor in others, prefers conifer woodland to deciduous, occasional elsewhere e.g. orchards. Rare: an excellent find.

SPARROWHAWK *Accipiter nisus*
Medium: 30–40 cm

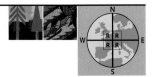

Agile hawk, a sprinter among birds of prey. Male grey above, white densely barred chestnut below, looks red. The much larger female is grey-brown above, white below with broad brown barring. Distinct white eyebrow. Immatures like female, but dark-streaked, not barred. Short round wings and long narrow tail show well in flight. Solitary.

Call: usually only in spring and summer, 'kee-kee-kee'. **Where?** Year-round in many woods, also hunting across farmland. Widespread but not numerous: a good spot.

GREAT SPOTTED WOODPECKER *Dendrocopos major*
Small: 23 cm

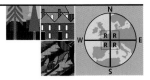

Typical woodpecker, climbing head-up on trees, with deep roller-coaster flight showing large white patches on wings. Barred black and white on back. Adult crown black, red patch on nape in male, all-red in immatures. Underparts white with characteristic red undertail. Usually solitary. **Call:** loud, sharp 'kek'. In spring, drums on dead wood,

lower-pitched and briefer than Lesser Spotted. **Where?** Year-round woodland resident, also on farmland. Visits village and suburban garden bird tables in winter. Fairly common.

LESSER SPOTTED WOODPECKER *Dendrocopos minor*
Small: 15 cm

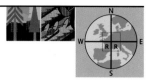

Sparrow-sized black and white barred woodpecker. Black and white head pattern; male has red crown, female white, immature reddish. Underparts white with no red below tail. Roller-coaster flight shows barred wings without white patches. Usually solitary.
Call: high-pitched 'kee-kee-kee'; drumming in spring higher pitched than Great Spotted, lasts longer.

Where? Deciduous woodland year-round, occasionally parks, orchards and farmland. Not common: a good find.

LONG-TAILED TIT *Aegithalos caudatus*
Tiny: 13 cm

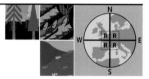

Unmistakable. Has the smallest body of any of our birds, spherical and fluffy, with a tail over half its length. Black and white head and wings, and white-edged black tail; pinkish buff back. Underparts whitish, tinged pink. Stubby black beak. Agile and acrobatic on twigs. Almost always in noisy family parties, flying from bush to bush one after the other, short rounded wings beating frantically.

Call: high-pitched 'tsee-tsee-tsee', deeper 'tuck', rattling 'cherrr'.
Where? Year-round resident on heathland, also in woodland, large gardens and on farmland. Fairly common, but always well worth watching.

TREE PIPIT *Anthus trivialis*
Small: 15 cm

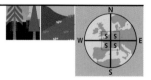

Long-legged pipit with distinctive parachuting song-flight. Yellow-brown above with plenty of darker streaks, buff below with dark streaks, whitish on belly. Legs pink. Usually solitary or in pairs.
Call: in flight distinctive 'tee-zee'; song a musical descending trill with a final flourish of 'zeee-arrr' notes.

Where? Summer visitor, the typical pipit of woodland clearings. Returns regularly to favoured woods, but not common.

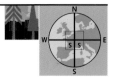

NIGHTINGALE *Luscinia megarhynchos*
Small: 17 cm

Drab small thrush but a wonderful singer. Adult brown, slightly paler below, with a reddish long tail. Immature has reddish tail, otherwise brown with buff spots like a young Robin. Usually solitary.
Call: quiet 'hooo-eet' call; magnificent varied musical song includes mimicking other birds and cello-like phrases; can go on and on, day and night.

Where? Summer visitor to deciduous woodland with dense undergrowth. Returns regularly to favoured woods each summer.

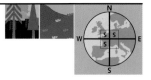

REDSTART *Phoenicurus phoenicurus*
Small: 15 cm

Small woodland thrush with distinctive dark-centred reddish tail. Male grey above with white forehead; underparts rich orange apart from black throat. Male in autumn and female browner and duller, immature brown with buff spots, but always with the characteristic tail. Usually solitary.
Call: soft 'whoo-eet' of alarm; brief tuneful song ending in a distinctive rattle.

Where? Regular summer visitor to woodland in the west and to birch scrub in the north, occasional migrant in other parts.

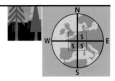

GARDEN WARBLER *Sylvia borin*
Small: 15 cm

Rather plump, dull olive above, paler below with no distinctive marks. Fairly stout black beak for a warbler, characteristic bluish legs. Usually solitary.
Call: sharp 'tchack' of alarm; beautiful song from deep in undergrowth, even compares well with Nightingale.

Where? Widespread in deciduous woodland with thick undergrowth and dense tall scrub; rarely numerous but not uncommon.

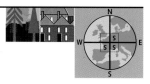

BLACKCAP *Sylvia atricapilla*
Small: 15 cm

Distinctively capped warbler: male olive brown, grey on underparts, with black cap. Female duller with brown cap. Immature has chestnut cap. Legs brown. Usually, but not always, solitary.
Call: sharp 'tchack' of alarm; tuneful song but less musical than Garden Warbler, and often briefer, ending on a rising note.

Where? Mostly a summer visitor, widespread in deciduous woodland and parks. Visits town gardens and bird tables in winter. Fairly common in summer, rare in winter.

WOOD WARBLER *Phylloscopus sibilatrix*
Tiny: 13 cm

Typical 'leaf warbler', called that because it lives mostly among the leaves of tree canopies, but larger than most others. Yellowish green upperparts, with a striking yellow stripe over eye; yellow throat and distinctive brilliant white belly. Usually solitary.
Call: flute-like 'dee-you' call; trilling song very distinctive, based on 'sip' notes, sliding down the scale getting faster and faster.

Often sings in parachuting song flight.
Where? Summer visitor to tall deciduous woodland, usually with little undergrowth. Not very common in most areas.

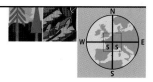

CHIFFCHAFF *Phylloscopus collybita*
Tiny: 10 cm

Small dull leaf warbler, plump and active. Olive above, grey-buff below often tinged yellow in immatures. Legs usually black (*see* similar Willow Warbler), beak tiny and pointed. Usually solitary.
Call: sorrowful 'whoo-eet'; song is easiest way of identifying, an apparently endless series of 'chiff' and 'chaff' notes.

Where? Mostly a summer visitor to tall woodland and parkland, occasionally stays over winter. Fairly common.

WILLOW WARBLER *Phylloscopus trochilus*
Tiny: 10 cm

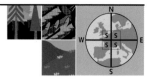

Small leaf warbler, with olive-green upperparts and a whitish stripe over eye. Underparts whitish, tinged yellow in immatures. Less usually pale brown (*see* Chiffchaff). Beak tiny. Usually solitary.

Call: too-eet call more positive than Chiffchaff; distinctive melodious song, a descending trill of silvery notes finishing with a flourish.

Where? Summer visitor to woodland and scrub (Chiffchaff prefers tall trees). Fairly common.

GOLDCREST *Regulus regulus*
Tiny: 9 cm

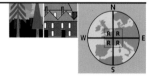

Like a warbler, small and plump with a tiny beak, this is the smallest bird in Europe. Olive-green above, whitish below. Double white wingbar on greenish wings. Distinctive black-edged gold stripe on crown, more orange in male, lacking in immatures. Sometimes in groups.

Call: characteristic very high pitched 'tzeee' call; song also very high pitched descending series of 'see' notes ending in a flourish.

Where? Year-round visitor to woodland, particularly conifers. Also parks and gardens. Not uncommon except after severely cold winters.

MARSH TIT *Parus palustris*
Tiny: 12 cm

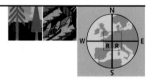

Black-capped tit. Upperparts brown, crown and nape black, cheeks whitish. Underparts grey with black bib. Very similar Willow Tit, *Parus montanus*, has bigger bib, thicker neck and a pale patch in its wings. Usually solitary.

Call: Marsh calls an abrupt 'pit-chew', Willow a thin 'dee' or 'zee'.The call is the best way of distinguishing one from the other.

Where? Both black-capped tits favour deciduous woodland, and are good finds as patchily distributed and scarce or rare almost everywhere.

CRESTED TIT *Parus cristatus*
Tiny: 12 cm

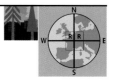

Only European tit with a crest. Brown above, whitish below. Distinctive black and white cheeks, black and white check pattern on pointed crest. Solitary or in small groups.
Call: song a high-pitched sequence of 'tzee' notes; purring call.

Where? In Britain, old highland Scottish pine forest year-round. Restricted but locally not uncommon: worth a journey to see it. More widespread in Europe.

COAL TIT *Parus ater*
Tiny: 12 cm

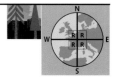

Agile tree-top tit. Back grey, wings and tail dark brown. Buff below, often chestnut on flanks. Distinctive head, with black bib, white cheeks, black crown with bold white square on nape. Flocks in winter.
Call: high-pitched 'tseet call'; song a series of 'wheat-see' notes.

Where? Year-round woodland resident, particularly likes conifers. Often visits town gardens and bird tables in winter. Fairly common.

PIED FLYCATCHER *Ficedula hypoleuca*
Tiny: 13 cm

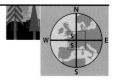

Plump flycatcher, male black above with white forehead, white below. Wings black with white bar, tail black edged white. Autumn male, female and immature have same patterns, but in dull brown above, grey below. Flies out from perch to catch insects with a snap of the beak. Solitary. Spotted Flycatcher, *Muscicapa striata*, is slimmer, brown plumage streaked black.

Call: sharp 'wit' of alarm; short scratchy song.
Where? Summer visitor to deciduous woodland. Spotted favours parks and gardens as well as woodland clearings. Both are only locally fairly common.

TREECREEPER *Certhia familiaris*
Tiny: 12 cm

Mouse-like creeper up tree trunks. Brown above with black and buff flecks, white below. Long slim and pointed downcurved beak, large eye under whitish stripe. Long stiff tail used as prop while climbing. In roller-coaster flight shows broad wingbars on rounded wings. Usually solitary. Very similar short-toed Treecreeper C*erthia brachydactyla* is common across Europe.

Call: thin but penetrating 'tseew'. High-pitched song of descending notes with a final flourish.
Where? Year-round resident in woodlands of all sorts, also parks, farmland and gardens with large trees. Widespread but not numerous. A good spot.

JAY *Garrulus glandarius*
Medium: 35 cm

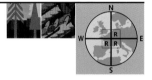

Colourful woodland crow, shy but conspicuous. Pinkish body with brown-streaked crown, black moustache and pale pink eye. Black and white wings with bright blue shoulder patch. Black tail and white rump conspicuous in floppy flight. Powerful slightly hooked beak. Usually solitary.

Call: strident 'skark'; soft warbling song rarely heard.
Where? Year-round resident in woodland, also farmland and parks. Not uncommon.

TREE SPARROW *Passer montanus*
Tiny: 13 cm

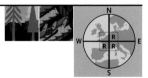

Small but chunky sparrow. Upperparts brown with darker streaks, whitish below. Characteristic head pattern with brown cap and white cheeks with black central spots. Small black bib, dark stubby beak. Fast flying. Often in small flocks.
Call: liquid 'chip, chup' or 'teck' in flight, with practice quite different from House Sparrow.

Where? Breeds in deciduous woodland, often winters on farmland nearby. Unlike House Sparrow, keeps away from people.

REDPOLL *Carduelis flammea*
Tiny: 12 cm

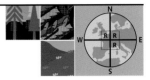

Tiny dark finch, brown with blackish streaks above, buff below. Small black bib and dark stubby beak. Distinctive red patch on forehead absent in immatures. Often in flocks, especially in winter.
Call: 'chee-chee-chit' and long 'sweee' in flight. Distinctive trilling song produced in circling flight high overhead.

Where? Year-round resident, breeding in woodland, spending the winter on weedy fields and feeding in waterside alder trees. Usually quite scarce: a good spot.

CROSSBILL *Loxia curvirostra*
Small: 16 cm

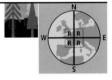

Bulky big-headed finch with large parrot-like beak crossed at tips – visible at close range. Male dull red with black wings, female and immature dull green, yellowish on rump. Clambers around conifers like a parrot, sometimes upside down. Often in small flocks.
Call: characteristic loud 'jup' or 'jip' calls; fast twittering and jangling song.

Where? Can turn up almost anywhere year-round in the conifer woods it prefers. Generally not at all common: a good and interesting spot.

HAWFINCH *Coccothraustes coccothraustes*
Small: 18 cm

Largest finch with massive head and beak. Brown above, buff below, with grey head. Diagnostic huge wedge-shaped silver beak. In roller-coaster flight shows white-tipped tail and striking white wingbars. Sometimes in flocks.
Call: sharp Robin-like 'tzick'; quiet chattering, warbling song rarely heard.

Where? Year-round resident in deciduous woodland, also in parks and orchards (especially damsons) in winter. Scarce and very shy and secretive: an excellent spot.

HEATHLAND

Heathland is the name given to areas of short bushes, bracken, heather and other plants. Trees are few and far between, and stunted, and there are many patches of bare earth or short grass nibbled short by rabbits, sheep and ponies. Often the soil is sandy, chalky or very stony, making it difficult for plants to grow. Those that do, and the beautiful yellow-flowered gorse is a good example, are often prickly (to protect themselves from grazing animals) and very dense. So birdwatching is not as easy as you might think. Many heathland and scrub birds spend much of the time skulking out of sight. Patience is needed, for sooner or later a bird will show itself, and others will come out to feed on the short grass. Always walk slowly, pausing often to look and listen. Sometimes you can encourage these skulking birds to show themselves by making squeaking noises with the back of your hand against your lips. Try it and see if it works.

HEN HARRIER *Circus cyaneus*
Medium: 40–50 cm

Distinctive in flight, gliding low with few flaps, long narrow wings with fingered tips held at right angles to body, long narrow tail. Male grey above with white rump, white below. Wings grey with black tips. The larger female and the immature brown have darker streaking and owl-like face patterns. White rump conspicuous in flight. Usually solitary, may gather in groups to roost.

Call: excited 'chuck-uk-uk-uk' (male) and 'kek-ek-ek-ek' (female) in nesting season.
Where? Year-round resident on heathland, also moorland, young forest plantations and marshes. Scarce – an exciting find and enjoyable to watch.

MERLIN *Falco columbarius*
Medium: 30 cm

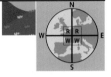

Small fast-flying falcon specializing in low-level attacks on small birds. Male slate grey above, buff with darker streaks below. The slightly larger female and the immature are mottled brown above, whitish below with heavy brown streaks. Compact and agile in flight, with pointed wings. Usually solitary.
Call: 'kikikikiki . . .' near nest

Where? Scarce anywhere and sadly getting scarcer. Year-round resident, can be summer only or winter only, on heathland, also moorland and hill farmland, marshes in winter. A great find.

HOBBY *Falco subbuteo*
Medium: 35 cm

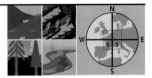

Fast and longest-winged falcon, Swift-like with slim wings. Adults grey above, with white collar and throat, black cap and facial streaks. Underparts white with dark streaks, thighs and undertail chestnut. Female is larger. Immature browner, lacks chestnut. Solitary.
Call: 'kew-kew-kew' or 'kikikiki' like Lesser Spotted Woodpecker, usually only near nest.

Where? Summer visitor to heathland with occasional trees, also to farmland. Often hunts Swallows and Martins over lakes near its nest. Uncommon: a super sighting.

STONE CURLEW *Burhinus oedicnemus*
Medium: 40 cm

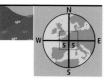

Strange wader or shore-bird but found on dry heathland and stony fields. Extremely well camouflaged, shy and often motionless during the day, active and noisy at night. Brown above with fine darker streaking, paler and streaked below. Short yellow and black beak, large yellow unblinking eyes. Legs long, yellow, with 'knobbly knees'. Shows bold black and white wingbar in flight. Solitary.

Call: 'kee-ooo' and 'kroo-lee' calls, and strange vibrating shrieks, always after dark.
Where? Summer visitor to heathland and farmland with wide-open spaces and few plants. Rare, very difficult to see so an excellent spot.

CUCKOO *Cuculus canorus*
Medium: 33 cm

Looks falcon-like in flight with long tail and pointed wings. Grey above, with grey wings and white-edged grey tail. Throat grey, rest of underparts white with black barring. Short beak yellow with black tip, short legs yellow. Immature browner, head and back barred grey. Lays its eggs in other birds' nests. Usually in ones or twos.
Call: best-known of all bird calls: 'cuck-oo', but sometimes gets mixed up if excited. Male also has throaty chuckle, female a fast bubbling trill.
Where? Summer heathland visitor, also farmland, woodland and moorland. Widespread, quite common.

GREEN WOODPECKER *Picus viridis*
Medium: 30 cm

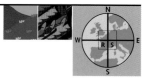

Typical shape, with long stiff tail and strong pale dagger beak, but spends most of its time on the ground feeding. Greenish gold back, whitish underparts. Red crown and nape, black face, moustachial streaks black in female, black and red in male. Immature duller and barred all over, lacks black face and moustaches. Looks short-legged.

Conspicuously roller-coaster flight. Usually in ones or twos.
Call: distinctive far-carrying laughing 'yah-yah-yah' or 'pew-pew-pew'.
Where? Widespread on heathland, also short grassland and woodland clearings. Often not uncommon.

MEADOW PIPIT *Anthus pratensis*
Small: 15 cm

Spends much of its time on the ground. Runs swiftly. Well camouflaged, brownish above, buff below, heavily streaked. White-edged tail visible in flight. Rock Pipit, *Anthus petrosus*, is larger and greyer, found along rocky coasts. Often in groups or flocks in winter.

Call: plaintive 'tseeep'. Trilling song produced in parachuting display flight.

Where? Heathland, farmland and moorland in summer, almost anywhere in winter. Widespread, quite common in places.

WOODLARK *Lullula arborea*
Small: 15 cm

Plump and distinctively short-tailed for a lark. Well camouflaged, dark brown above with dark and pale flecks, buff below with dark-streaked breast. Striped crown, clear whitish stripe over eye, pale edges to dark cheeks. No crest. Shows white on shoulders of wings in flight. Usually solitary.

Call: useful and easily remembered 'too-loo-eet' or 'tee-loo-eee' in flight; musical flute-like song with 'loo-loo-lee' phrases.

Where? Summer visitor to heathland, woodland clearings. Pretty scarce and a good find.

YELLOWHAMMER *Emberiza citrinella*
Small: 18 cm

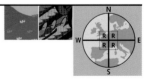

Typical rather long bunting, with wedge-shaped beak. Summer male chestnut with dark streaks on back, bright yellow head, yellow breast with chestnut streaks. Winter male, female and immature duller and browner, with streaked head pattern, but still with some yellow on head and underparts. White-edged tail shows in flight. Solitary in summer, flocks in winter.

Call: 'chwick' in flight; easily remembered song a series of 'zit' notes ending with a long 'tzeeee'.

Where? Widespread year-round on heathland, also farmland. Fairly common in many areas.

WHINCHAT *Saxicola rubetra*
Tiny: 13 cm

Plump, upright, short-tailed small thrush with long slim legs, usually perched on bush tops flicking wings and tail non-stop. Spring male mottled brown above, with blackish crown and white stripe over eye. Underparts orange. Autumn male, female and immature duller, but all show characteristic white patches at base of tail. Usually solitary.

Call: 'tcheck'; brief scratchy warbling song, usually in flight. **Where?** Summer visitor to heathland, occasional also on farmland. Usually scarce, therefore a good spot.

STONECHAT *Saxicola torquata*
Tiny: 13 cm

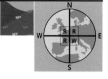

Plump, dark short-tailed thrush with long slim legs, usually perched on bush tops flicking wings and tail non-stop. Summer male very dark brown above, with black face and white collar. Underparts rusty red. Winter male, female and immature duller and browner, still orange on breast. Shows white in wings in flight. Solitary or in family groups. **Call:** sharp 'tchack', brief scratchy warble of a song.

Where? Widespread year-round resident on heathland, also around the coast, on moorland and occasionally on farmland. Not usually common; fun birds to watch.

WHEATEAR *Oenanthe oenanthe*
Small: 15 cm

Usually easiest identified at all times by distinctive white upside-down 'U' patch on rump and tail clearly visible in flight. Summer male pale grey above, apricot below, with black eyepatch, wings and tail. Autumn male, female and immature much duller and browner, immature also speckled. Solitary or in small groups.

Call: sharp 'chack' call; brief scratchy song, usually in flight. **Where?** Widespread on heathland, also moorland and round the coast, occasionally on migration on farmland. Widespread but not very common, a good find.

DARTFORD WARBLER *Sylvia undata*
Tiny: 13 cm

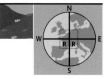

An unusual warbler, not migrating south for the winter. Also very dark, short-winged and long-tailed. Male dark grey above, with white tip to long tail which is often cocked. Dark maroon breast, grey belly. White flecks in throat, red eye ring. Finely pointed beak. Legs orange. Female and immature duller. Secretive, stays deep in undergrowth. Usually in ones or twos.

Call: loud 'chuck' and scolding 'churr'; scratchy warbling song, usually in flight.
Where? Year-round resident in a few areas of gorsey heath, numbers fall sharply after snowy winters. Not uncommon where it does occur – worth travelling to see.

WHITETHROAT *Sylvia communis*
Small: 15 cm

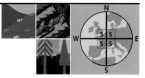

Summer male has chestnut wings, brown back, grey head, pinkish breast and white throat. Autumn male, female and immature duller, but all have white-edged tail and pale throats. Lesser Whitethroat, *Sylvia curruca*, is smaller, grey above, pinkish-grey below, with dark patch through eye, favours farmland and woodland clearings.
Call: 'tchack' call (soft 'tack' for Lesser); scratchy song produced in bouncy flight (Lesser has monotonous dry rattle).
Where? Summer visitor to heathland, also farmland hedges. Once very common, now less common but still widespread. Lesser widespread, but quite scarce and unobtrusive.

LINNET *Carduelis cannabina*
Small: 14 cm

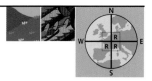

Small finch always twittering noisily. Male has chestnut back, grey head with red forehead, pink breast and buff belly, all duller and hidden by scaly markings in winter. Female brown, with greyish head, no pink; immature duller still. All have black wings with white feather edges, white-edged blackish tail. Triangular black beak. Usually in flocks.

Call: loud 'sweet' and 'chwee' in flight; twittering but musical song.
Where? Widespread year-round on heathland, also farmland, woodland clearings and large weedy gardens and allotments. Often quite common.

FRESHWATERS

Freshwater habitats come in all shapes and sizes, each with a group of birds that like to use it for swimming, feeding, and even nesting. The grebe family, for example, build floating raft-like nests of waterweed and lay their eggs on top. Even the smallest pond in a city centre park will have Mallard and Moorhen, while ducks and grebes like large lakes and reservoirs (especially in winter). Fast-flowing clear water streams cascading over pebbles and rocks attract Dippers and Grey Wagtails, while the spectacular Kingfisher prefers slower-moving water. Smaller waterside birds find their home in the reeds. Many are well camouflaged, so wait and listen for clues as to what is there.

Water birds often feel safe out on the water, so may be quite approachable. Always keep your eyes open, because other birds (Swifts, Swallows and Martins) often gather over freshwater to feed on the masses of insects.

LITTLE GREBE *Tachybaptus ruficollis*
Medium: 25 cm

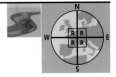

Often called Dabchick. Smallest and dumpiest grebe, dives frequently. Distinctive tail-less appearance, with short neck and small head. In summer dark brown above with chestnut face and neck, duller brown in winter. White on belly. Short dark triangular beak, fleshy yellow patch at base. Lobed toes on feet set back near tail. Needs long take-off run, pattering across water, but usually dives to escape danger. Solitary or small groups.
Call: distinctive whinnying song in spring.
Where? Widespread year-round on lakes, reservoirs and slow-moving rivers and overgrown canals. Fairly common.

GREAT CRESTED GREBE *Podiceps cristatus*
Medium: 45 cm

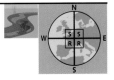

Largest grebe, almost twice the size of Dabchick. Dives neatly and often. Slim, long necked, with distinctive chestnut and buff crested head and long dagger-shaped beak. Looks tail-less. Grey-brown above, white below, white neck. Shows white wing patches in flight. Lobed toes. Long pattering take-off run. Solitary or in small groups.

Call: occasional harsh 'croaks' in spring. Young have penetrating piping whistle.
Where? Widespread year-round on larger lakes, reservoirs etc.; rarely on rivers but occasional on sheltered seas in winter. Common.

GREY HERON *Ardea cinerea*
Huge: 95 cm

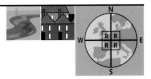

Well-known long-necked long-legged waterbird. Grey above, white below, with black crown and long drooping crest, black markings down slim throat. Yellowish beak long and dagger-shaped. Immature duller. Looks huge in flight, wings long and broad, fingered at tips, legs trailing, head and neck characteristically folded back between shoulders. Stands motionless in water waiting for fish prey. Usually solitary, but nests in treetop colonies.
Call: harsh honking 'frank'.
Where? Widespread year-round beside freshwater, occasional on the seashore. Fairly common.

BITTERN *Botaurus stellaris*
Large: 70 cm

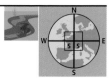

Wonderfully camouflaged heron, brown with buff and black streaks, looks exactly like reed stems. Usually has neck tucked down. Longish dagger-shaped beak, long legs greenish. In flight looks like smaller rounder-winged dark Grey Heron. Secretive. Usually solitary. **Call:** unique foghorn-like booming 'oo-wumph', carries long distances. More often heard than seen.

Where? Rare summer visitor to a handful of really large reedbeds. Extremely shy and difficult to spot: an excellent sighting.

CORMORANT *Phalacrocorax carbo*
Huge: 90 cm

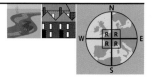

Broad-winged, blackish with greenish sheen, adults with white face and (sometimes) large white spot on flank absent in duller immatures. Long slim yellowish beak with powerful hooked tip. Swims low on the water, longish tail flat on the surface, dives often. Flies in 'V' formation. Sometimes perches with wings out at right angles drying off. Solitary or in groups.

Call: growling calls in breeding season.
Where? At home year-round on freshwater lakes, reservoirs etc., also on the coast. Fairly common, increasingly so inland.

MUTE SWAN *Cygnus olor*
Huge: 150 cm

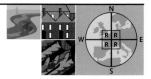

Unmistakable swan. All-white, with orange-red beak with black knob at base. Neck held in a graceful 'S'. Often raises its wings like sails when swimming to defend its territory. Immature buffish grey, becomes white with age. Aggressive. Long take-off run. Wings huge and broad in flight, often creak as they beat. Solitary or in groups, often tame.

Call: not really 'mute', occasional grunts and hisses.
Where? Widespread year-round on lakes anywhere, even city centres, reservoirs with vegetation, slow-moving rivers; occasionally on the sea in winter. Common.

WHOOPER SWAN *Cygnus cygnus*
Huge: 150 cm

Unmistakably a swan, all-white but carries its neck stiff and straight. Beak wedge-shaped, yellow and black. Immatures buff, becoming white with age. Similar Bewick's Swan, *Cygnus columbianus*, also has straight neck but is smaller (120 cm) with less yellow on beak. Both are really wild swans. Usually in flocks. **Call:** Whooper gives noisy wild, whooping, trumpetting, calls; Bewick's also noisy, with honking, barking calls.

Where? Both wild swans are winter visitors to remote lakes and other wetlands, and to fields and marshes nearby. Scarce, but regular each winter: both are a wonderful sight.

CANADA GOOSE *Branta canadensis*
Huge: 100 cm

Largest and most familiar goose. Body brown, paler on belly, white undertail. Head and long neck black with distinctive white cheeks and chin. Wings broad and all-dark in flight, rump and tail banded black and white. Beak and legs black. Often in flocks. **Call:** characteristically a noisy gabbling 'aar-honk' call.

Where? Introduced into Britain and Europe from North America, now widespread year-round and increasing in numbers. Favours freshwaters of all shapes and sizes, even in city centres. Common.

COMMON TERN *Sterna hirundo*
Medium: 35 cm

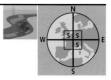

Called 'sea swallows' for good reasons. Slim bodied, with long slender wings and deeply forked tail, they are almost as agile in flight as real Swallows. White body, grey back and wings, black cap. Red beak with black tip, shortish red legs. Dive for food from several metres above the water. Sometimes solitary, sometimes in groups.

Call: distinctive rasping 'kee-arrr', rapid-fire 'kirri-kirri-kirri'.
Where? Summer visitor particularly to large water-filled gravel pits inland; also common along the coast.

GADWALL *Anas strepera*
Medium: 50 cm

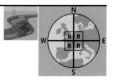

Surface-feeding (rather than diving) duck, typical duck shape, beak and webbed feet. Male greyish, characteristically black under tail, female and immature speckled brown. In flight both sexes show conspicuous black and white patch on the trailing edge of the wing. Upends to feed. Often in pairs, rarely in flocks.

Call: normally silent, but male has quiet whistle, female a 'quack'.
Where? Year-round resident on freshwater marshes, larger lakes and gravel pits. Widespread but uncommon, a good spot.

TEAL *Anas crecca*
Medium: 35 cm

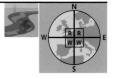

Smallest surface-feeding duck, fast and agile in flight. Male has chestnut head with dark green patch round eye, mottled grey-brown back, buff breast. Distinctive black and white stripe separates flanks from back. Yellow undertail. Female and immature also distinctively small, mottled grey-brown. Feeds along water's edge. Often in flocks, especially in winter.

Call: male has a characteristic 'krit-krit' and a bell-like whistle, female a 'quack'.
Where? Widespread, often common, on larger freshwaters and marshes in winter, also on estuaries and the sea. Rare as breeding bird on marshes.

MALLARD *Anas platyrhynchos*
Large: 58 cm

By far the commonest duck. Surface-feeder, often upends to feed. Male has brown body, glossy green head, curly black and white tail. Greenish beak, orange legs and webbed feet. Female and immature speckled brown, with brown beak and brown-orange legs. In flight shows white-edged purple patch in wing. Often in flocks, often tame.

Call: male uses quiet whistle, female a harsh loud series of 'quacks'.
Where? Almost anywhere, anytime, from the smallest pond (even in city centres) to large lakes and the coast. Common.

TUFTED DUCK *Aythya fuligula*
Medium: 40 cm

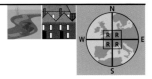

Small and unmistakable dumpy diving duck. Male black above, white below, purplish-black head with long drooping crest and yellow eye. Grey beak. Female and immature brown, paler below, sometimes with white on face. Fast in flight, shows striking white bars full length of wings. Dives neatly and frequently. Often in groups or flocks.

Call: usually quiet; male has soft whistle, female a low growl.
Where? Year-round resident, also winter visitor. Breeds on reed-edged lakes; winters on most types of freshwater, even in towns. Widespread, often common.

POCHARD *Aythya ferina*
Medium: 45 cm

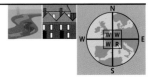

Distinctive diving duck. Male has grey body, black breast and tail, chestnut head with distinctive wedge-shaped profile. Female grey-brown, paler below, darker brown head and tail. In flight shows broad whitish bar along wing, not as clear as Tufted Duck. Usually in flocks in winter; seems to spend a lot of time dozing on the surface.

Call: usually silent: female may growl.
Where? Year-round resident in some areas, migrant in others. Numbers increase in winter. Breeds on large reed-edged lakes; winters on large freshwaters of all sorts. Only occasional on the coast.

WATER RAIL *Rallus aquaticus*
Medium: 28 cm

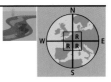

Ultra-shy but sometimes noisy reed-bed bird. Slim and skulking, it slips between the reeds, walking on long spidery toes that stop it sinking in the mud. Dark brown above with black markings, dark grey head and underparts with black and white barring on flanks. Beak long and slim, reddish and downcurved. Rarely flies, but does so with legs dangling. Usually solitary.

Call: often described, accurately, as like a squealing pig.
Where? Year-round resident, sometimes winter visitor, in large marshy and reed-bed areas. Scarce, more often heard than seen: a good find.

MOORHEN *Gallinula chloropus*
Medium: 35 cm

Brownish-black with characteristic white line on flanks, fleshy red forehead, yellow-tipped beak. White undertail conspicuous when swimming or walking, tail flicks non-stop. Long greenish legs with red 'garter', long spidery toes. Immature duller and browner, lacks fleshy forehead. Often swims, upending for food. Sometimes in groups.

Call: ringing calls include loud 'whittuck' and repeated 'kek'.
Where? Year-round resident on freshwaters of almost any size and type, almost anywhere including city park ponds. Widespread and fairly common.

COOT *Fulica atra*
Medium: 38 cm

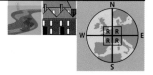

Larger and plumper than Moorhen, looks tail-less. Sooty black all over except for fleshy white forehead and white beak. Red eye, legs grey with distinctive lobed toes. Flies low over the water showing bright white trailing edge to wings. Aggressive – often dashes at other Coots, wings raised. Swims well, dives neatly for food. Often in scattered groups.

Call: usually an explosive 'kowk', also loud high 'pik'.
Where? Likes larger, more-open freshwaters than Moorhen. Widespread year-round, common.

MARSH HARRIER *Circus aeruginosus*
Large: 50–55 cm

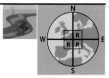

Typical harrier, often gliding low, long legs dangling, over reedbeds and marshes, broad wings held at right angles in a shallow 'V'; longish tail sometimes fanned. Male brown above, chestnut below, striking grey, black and brown patterned wings. The larger female is a rich brown with a lot of yellow on the head; immature duller, yellow absent. Often solitary.

Call: usually silent; loud 'kee-yaar' near nest.
Where? Likes freshwater marshes with areas of reedbed for nesting. Occurs in other habitats at times. Rare, but often returns to same areas to breed. An excellent spot.

OSPREY *Pandion haliaetus*
Large: 55-70 cm

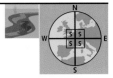

Distinctive 'fish-hawk', eagle-like in appearance, but diving with a spectacular splash for fish prey. The female is larger than the male. Dark brown above (with white barring in immatures), white below with a few darker streaks. Characteristic black and white head pattern, golden eye. Powerful grey feet: carries large fish head first like a torpedo. Usually solitary.

Call: plaintive whistling calls near nest.
Where? Summer visitor breeding beside lakes (treetop nest of branches and twigs), sometimes be seen on migration spring and autumn at any large freshwater. Rare: a superb and exciting sight.

KINGFISHER *Alcedo atthis*
Small: 17 cm

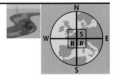

Long-beaked and dumpy, brilliantly coloured and unmistakable, but surprisingly difficult to see. Electric blue-green above, reddish chestnut below, long dagger-shaped beak all-black in male, reddish underneath in female. Tiny red feet. Head with barred blue crown, chestnut, blue and white face and throat pattern. Direct whirring flight. Usually solitary.

Call: well worth knowing, because you can then hear one coming – loud shrill 'zeee' or 'cheet'.
Where? Year-round resident beside streams, rivers and lakes, summer visitor in north. Not very common: a 'brilliant' sighting!

SAND MARTIN *Riparia riparia*
Tiny: 12 cm

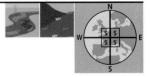

Small martin, sandy brown above, white below with a sandy collar band. Darting flight on slim curved wings, streamlined bullet-shaped body, short tail with a shallow notch. Usually seen in flight and usually in flocks.
Call: sharp 'chirrup of alarm', quiet trilling song in flight.

Where? Much less numerous than it used to be, but still a common migrant and summer visitor. Likes sandy soils (cliff edges to sand pits) to dig nest burrows. Often feeds over larger freshwater areas. Not widespread.

GREY WAGTAIL *Motacilla cinerea*
Small: 18 cm

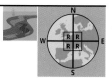

Longest-tailed of the wagtails, running beside the water with tail wagging non-stop. Grey above, with blackish wings and white-edged black tail. Whitish stripe over eye. White breast (male has a black bib in summer), distinctively lemon yellow on undertail. Immature duller and paler. Usually in ones and twos.
Call: characteristic high-pitched 'chee-seek' or 'tsee-tsit' call, song like Blue Tit, 'tsee tsee tsee' followed by a trill.
Where? Resident year-round beside fast moving streams, rapids, sluices. Quite scarce, an elegant bird and a good spot.

DIPPER *Cinclus cinclus*
Small: 17 cm

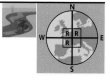

Like a large waterside Wren, dumpy and dark brown with a chestnut-edged white breast. Brown tail often held cocked up. Easily identified also by its behaviour, standing on a boulder midstream, bobbing up and down before walking right into and under the water to find food. Whirring flight on rounded wings low and straight over the water. Usually solitary.
Call: distinctive 'zit' gives early warning of its coming.
Where? Year-round resident beside clear, fast-flowing streams and rivers with plenty of rocks. Quite scarce: a good find and very interesting to watch.

REED BUNTING *Emberiza schoeniclus*
Small: 15 cm

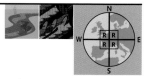

Summer male easily identified by black-streaked chestnut back, black head and striking white collar. White-edged black tail conspicuous in flight. Winter male, female and immature all similar and more difficult, generally mottled brown but with a characteristic brown and white head pattern. Often solitary, in flocks in winter.
Call: harsh 'tsee-you' call; jangling song produced from perch.
Where? Widespread year-round in damp marshy habitats and beside lakes, rivers and streams, occasionally on farmland in winter. Fairly common.

SEDGE WARBLER *Acrocephalus schoenobaenus*
Tiny: 13 cm

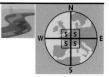

Noisy, heavily streaked brown wetland warbler, pale buff below, with dark-streaked crown and conspicuous whitish stripe over eye. Looks short winged with a rounded brown tail. Perches on upright stems to sing. Usually alone, but many may be dotted about the same marsh. Not shy. **Call:** sharp 'tchuck'. Song repetitive, 'churring' and metallic, often with snatches of imitations.

Where? Summer visitor to swamps, marshes, reedbeds, moist areas with dense vegetation. Widespread, fairly common.

REED WARBLER *Acrocephalus scirpaceus*
Tiny: 14 cm

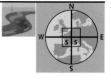

Noisy unstreaked brown wetland warbler, reddish brown above, buff below. Relatively long beak and flattish head, only faint paler stripe over eye. Rounded tail. Perches on reed stems to sing. Usually solitary, may be several dotted about the same reedbed. **Call:** scolding 'churr'; sings in longer bursts than Sedge, more musical, less harsh and without any imitations.

Where? Summer visitor to reedbeds, builds neat woven nest skilfully attached to a group of vertical reed stems. Common.

BEARDED TIT *Panurus biarmicus*
Small: 16 cm

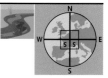

Reedbed acrobat, clambering agilely about the reed stems. Brown, with brown, black and white wings; white-edged tapered black, buff and white tail. Male has distinctive grey head with bushy black moustache, yellow eye. Female is browner, immature buffer, both lacking head pattern. Usually in groups, often tame.

Call: distinctive 'ping' calls and only a brief chattering song. **Where?** Migrant or resident, can turn up in large reedbeds almost anywhere. Numbers vary, but usually scarce. Always a good spot.

TOWN

BIRD	TOWN	FARM	WOOD	HEATH	FRESHWATER	NORTHWEST	NORTHEAST	SOUTHWEST	SOUTHEAST
HERRING GULL	•	-	-	-	•	R	R	R	R
LESSER BLACK-BACKED GULL	•	•	-	-	•	S	S	S	R
GREAT BLACK-BACKED GULL	•	-	-	-	•	S	R	R	R
BLACK-HEADED GULL	•	•	-	-	•	R	R	R	R
WOODPIGEON	•	•	•	•	-	R	R	R	R
COLLARED DOVE	•	•	-	-	-	R	R	R	R
SWIFT	•	•	-	•	•	S	S	S	S
SWALLOW	•	•	-	•	•	S	S	S	S
HOUSE MARTIN	•	-	-	•	•	S	S	S	S
PIED WAGTAIL	•	•	-	-	•	R	R	R	R
WREN	•	•	•	•	-	R	R	R	R
DUNNOCK	•	•	•	•	-	R	R	R	R
ROBIN	•	•	•	-	-	R	R	R	R
BLACKBIRD	•	•	•	•	-	R	R	R	R
SONG THRUSH	•	•	•	•	-	R	R	R	R
MISTLE THRUSH	•	•	•	-	-	R	R	R	R
BLUE TIT	•	•	•	-	-	R	R	R	R
GREAT TIT	•	•	•	-	-	R	R	R	R
STARLING	•	•	•	-	-	R	R	R	R
MAGPIE	•	•	•	•	-	R	R	R	R
JACKDAW	•	•	•	-	-	R	R	R	R
HOUSE SPARROW	•	•	-	-	-	R	R	R	R
CHAFFINCH	•	•	•	-	-	R	R	R	R
GREENFINCH	•	•	•	•	-	R	R	R	R
SISKIN	•	•	-	-	•	R	R	R	W
GOLDFINCH	•	•	•	•	-	R	R	R	R
NUTHATCH	•	•	•	-	-	-	-	R	R

FARMLAND

BIRD	TOWN	FARM	WOOD	HEATH	FRESHWATER	NORTHWEST	NORTHEAST	SOUTHWEST	SOUTHEAST
PINK-FOOTED GOOSE	-	•	-	-	•	W	W	W	-
WHITE-FRONTED GOOSE	-	•	-	-	-	W	W	W	W
GREYLAG GOOSE	-	•	-	-	•	R	R	R	R
KESTREL	•	•	•	•	-	R	R	R	R
RED-LEGGED PARTRIDGE	-	•	-	•	-	-	-	-	R
GREY PARTRIDGE	-	•	-	•	-	-	R	R	R
QUAIL	-	•	-	•	-	-	-	S	S
PHEASANT	-	•	•	-	-	-	R	R	R
LAPWING	-	•	-	-	•	R	R	W	W
COMMON GULL	-	•	-	-	•	R	R	W	W
BARN OWL	-	•	-	-	-	R	R	R	R
LITTLE OWL	-	•	•	-	-	-	-	R	R
SKYLARK	-	•	-	•	-	R	R	R	R
FIELDFARE	-	•	•	-	-	W	S	W	W
REDWING	-	•	•	-	-	R	R	W	W
RAVEN	-	•	•	-	-	R	R	R	-
ROOK	-	•	•	-	-	R	R	R	R
CARRION/HOODED CROW	•	•	•	•	-	R	R	R	R
BRAMBLING	-	•	•	-	-	W	S	W	W
BULLFINCH	•	•	•	-	-	R	R	R	R
CORN BUNTING	-	•	-	•	-	R	R	R	R

WOODLAND

BIRD	TOWN	FARM	WOOD	HEATH	FRESHWATER	NORTHWEST	NORTHEAST	SOUTHWEST	SOUTHEAST
STOCK DOVE	-	•	•	•	-	-	R	R	R
TURTLE DOVE	-	•	•	•	-	-	-	S	S
TAWNY OWL	•	•	•	-	-	R	R	R	R
LONG-EARED OWL	-	-	•	-	-	W	R	W	R
SPARROWHAWK	-	•	•	-	-	R	R	R	R
GREAT SPOTTED WOODPECKER	•	•	•	-	-	R	R	R	R
LESSER SPOTTED WOODPECKER	-	•	•	-	-	-	-	R	R
LONG-TAILED TIT	-	•	•	•	-	R	R	R	R
TREE PIPIT	-	-	•	•	-	S	S	S	S
NIGHTINGALE	-	-	•	-	-	-	-	S	S
REDSTART	-	-	•	•	-	S	S	S	-
GARDEN WARBLER	-	-	•	-	-	-	S	S	S
BLACKCAP	•	-	•	-	-	-	S	S	S
WOOD WARBLER	-	-	•	-	-	S	S	S	-

BIRD	TOWN	FARM	WOOD	HEATH	FRESHWATER	NORTHWEST	NORTHEAST	SOUTHWEST	SOUTHEAST
CHIFFCHAFF	-	•	•	-	-	-	-	S	S
WILLOW WARBLER	-	•	•	•	-	S	S	S	S
GOLDCREST	•	-	•	-	-	R	R	R	R
MARSH TIT	-	•	•	-	-	-	-	R	R
CRESTED TIT	-	-	•	-	-	R	R	-	-
COAL TIT	-	-	•	-	-	R	R	R	R
PIED FLYCATCHER	-	-	•	-	-	S	-	S	-
TREECREEPER	-	•	•	-	-	R	R	R	R
JAY	-	•	•	-	-	-	R	R	R
TREE SPARROW	-	•	•	-	-	-	R	R	R
REDPOLL	-	•	•	•	-	R	R	-	R
CROSSBILL	-	-	•	-	-	R	R	R	R
HAWFINCH	-	•	•	-	-	-	-	R	R

BIRD	TOWN	FARM	WOOD	HEATH	FRESHWATER	NORTHWEST	NORTHEAST	SOUTHWEST	SOUTHEAST
HEN HARRIER	-	•	-	•	-	R	R	W	W
MERLIN	-	-	-	•	-	R	R	W	W
HOBBY	-	•	•	•	•	-	-	S	S
STONE CURLEW	-	-	-	•	-	-	-	S	S
CUCKOO	-	•	•	•	-	S	S	S	S
GREEN WOODPECKER	-	•	-	•	-	-	-	R	R
MEADOW PIPIT	-	•	-	•	-	R	R	R	R
WOODLARK	-	-	•	•	-	-	-	S	S
YELLOWHAMMER	-	•	-	•	-	R	R	R	R
WHINCHAT	-	•	-	•	-	S	S	S	-
STONECHAT	-	-	-	•	-	R	R	R	W
WHEATEAR	-	•	-	•	-	S	S	S	S
DARTFORD WARBLER	-	-	-	•	-	-	-	R	R

BIRD	TOWN	FARM	WOOD	HEATH	FRESHWATER	NORTHWEST	NORTHEAST	SOUTHWEST	SOUTHEAST
WHITETHROAT	-	•	•	•	-	S	S	S	S
LINNET	-	•	-	•	-	-	R	R	R

FRESHWATER

BIRD	TOWN	FARM	WOOD	HEATH	FRESHWATER	NORTHWEST	NORTHEAST	SOUTHWEST	SOUTHEAST
LITTLE GREBE	-	-	-	-	•	R	R	R	R
GREAT CRESTED GREBE	-	-	-	-	•	S	S	R	R
GREY HERON	•	-	-	-	•	R	R	R	R
BITTERN	-	-	-	-	•	-	-	S	S
CORMORANT	•	-	-	-	•	R	R	R	R
MUTE SWAN	•	•	-	-	•	R	R	R	R
WHOOPER SWAN	-	•	-	-	•	W	W	-	-
CANADA GOOSE	•	•	-	-	•	-	-	R	R
COMMON TERN	-	-	-	-	•	S	S	-	S
GADWALL	-	-	-	-	•	R	R	R	R
TEAL	-	-	-	-	•	R	R	W	W
MALLARD	•	•	-	-	•	R	R	R	R
TUFTED DUCK	•	-	-	-	•	R	R	R	R
POCHARD	•	-	-	-	•	W	W	W	R
WATER RAIL	-	-	-	-	•	-	R	R	R
MOORHEN	•	•	-	-	•	R	R	R	R
COOT	•	-	-	-	•	R	R	R	R
MARSH HARRIER	-	-	-	-	•	-	R	R	R
OSPREY	-	-	-	-	•	S	S	S	S
KINGFISHER	-	-	-	-	•	-	S	R	R
SAND MARTIN	-	-	-	•	•	S	S	S	S
GREY WAGTAIL	-	-	-	-	•	R	R	R	R
DIPPER	-	-	-	-	•	R	R	R	-
REED BUNTING	-	•	-	-	•	R	R	R	R
SEDGE WARBLER	-	-	-	-	•	S	S	S	S
REED WARBLER	-	-	-	-	•	-	-	S	S
BEARDED TIT	-	-	-	-	•	-	-	S	S

Now Read On . . .

There are masses of bird books, some describing all the birds of the world in several very expensive, lavish volumes, others telling you just about all there is to know about only one species, and yet more telling you how and where birds live. This book is designed for young birdwatchers just starting on a fascinating hobby.

FIELD GUIDES

More information in greater detail is given in many field guides: two popular ones are

A Kingfisher prepares to plunge

> *Birds of Europe* by Lars Jonsson, published in paperback by Christopher Helm. The author also painted the superb illustrations, but if you prefer photographs of birds for more reality, then try *Photographic Field Guide: Birds of Britain and Europe* by Jim Flegg and David Hosking, published by New Holland.

Bird Songs and Calls of Britain and Europe by Geoff Sample, is accompanied by two audio CDs. Published by Harper Collins, it is immensely helpful in the vital business of learning songs and calls. For where to go birdwatching, details of over 400 excellent places are given in Collins *Top Birding Spots in Britain and Ireland* by David Tipling, published by Harper Collins. For those staying at home the *Pocket Birdfeeder Handbook* by Robert Burton, published by Dorling Kindersley, gives lots of helpful hints on how to tempt more birds into your garden.

The very latest guides, of course, are on CD-ROMs giving text, still and video illustrations, plus sound recordings, that run through a PC. Send for details of current versions to Birdguides, Jack House, Sheffield S36 4ZA, UK.

CLUBS AND SOCIETIES TO JOIN:

Marsh Harriers

The Royal Society for the Protection of Birds – The Lodge, Sandy, Bedfordshire SG19 2DL – is the bird conservation organisation. It has local Members' Groups all over Britain, probably one near you, and publishes an excellent magazine. The RSPB runs the Young Ornithologists' Club – the YOC – also with branches and organized outings locally as well as nationally.

The British Trust for Ornithology – The Nunnery, Thetford, Norfolk IP24 2PU – is the organisation for really serious birdwatchers who want to help with surveys, censuses and other studies like bird ringing.

The Wildlife Trust – The Green, Witham Park, Waterside South, Lincoln LN5 7JR – is the organisation to contact if you want to help more directly with conservation. The trust owns and maintains local nature reserves across the country.

Many counties and some major cities and towns have their own birdwatching clubs: your local library will be pleased to give you addresses.

INDEX